Little Mitchie

LET'S LOOK INSIDE A BADGER'S DEN

TRACY VONDER BRINK

LET'S LOOK INSIDE: ANIMAL HOMES

CREATING YOUNG NONFICTION READERS

Little Mitchie books spark curiosity and support early nonfiction reading for students in Grades 2-3. Designed to build vocabulary, support second language learners, and prepare readers for middle-grade content, each book includes helpful tips for parents and educators to build confidence and deepen understanding of the world.

TIPS FOR READING NONFICTION WITH BEGINNING READERS

Talk about Nonfiction

Begin by explaining that nonfiction books give us information that is true. The book will be organized around a specific topic or idea, and we may learn new facts through reading.

Look at the Parts

Most nonfiction books have helpful features. Our *Little Mitchie* titles include color photographs and graphic aids, a table of contents, a glossary, and an index. Share the purpose of these features with your reader.

Color Photos and Graphic Aids

A lot of information can be found by "reading" photos, charts, maps, and other graphic aids found within nonfiction texts. Help your reader learn more about the different ways information can be displayed.

Table of Contents

Located at the front of the book, this list shows the big ideas within the text and the page numbers where they can be found.

Glossary

Located at the back of the book, the glossary defines key words and phrases that are related to the topic. These words and phrases can be found in the text in colored type.

Index

Located at the back of the book, an index is an alphabetical list of topics and the page numbers where they can be found.

With a little help and guidance about reading nonfiction, you can feel good about introducing a young reader to the world of *Little Mitchie* nonfiction books.

Little Mitchie is an imprint of:

Mitchell Lane
PUBLISHERS

2001 SW 31st Avenue
Hallandale, FL 33009
mitchelllanepub.com

First Edition, 2027.

Author: Tracy Vonder Brink
Designer: Jen Bowers
Editor: Tricia Hoffman

Library of Congress Cataloging-in-Publication Data
Title: Let's Look Inside a Badger's Den /
by Tracy Vonder Brink

Description: Hallandale, FL :
Mitchell Lane Publishers, [2027]

Identifiers:
ISBN 979-8-89260-876-3 (library bound)
ISBN 979-8-89260-973-9 (eBook)

Library of Congress Control Number: 2026936531

PHOTO CREDITS
Shutterstock: cover, p.1 ©2022 Elizabeth Caron, p.5 ©2013 Frank L Junior, p.6 ©2016 Holly Kuchera, p.9 ©2019 David OBrien, p.11 ©2021 MelaniWright, p.12–13 ©2022 Dennis Laughlin, p.14–15 ©2013 Cynthia Kidwell, p.16 ©2011 Max Allen, p.19 ©2022 Dennis Laughlin, p.20–21 ©2019 FotoRequest, p.22 ©Fona, © YG Studio

TABLE OF CONTENTS

Chapter One

BURROWING BADGERS

American badgers are built to dig. They spend most of their lives underground in **burrows** that are sometimes called dens. Their paws work like shovels to scoop out dirt. What's it like inside a badger's den?

HOME SWEET HOME

American badgers live in open areas like grasslands and at the edges of woods. They're found from California to Ohio.

American badgers are **solitary**. Each builds many burrows every year. Large dens may be 10 feet (3 m) underground and have as many as 33 feet (10 m) of tunnels. Badgers use dens for sleeping, hunting, storing food, and having young.

Chapter Two

PARTS OF A BADGER'S DEN

Dens usually have one or two entrances. Badgers push out soil as they dig, so a burrow's entrance has a pile of soil around it. The entrances lead to tunnels. The tunnels connect to a **chamber**. Many dens only have one chamber.

HOME SWEET HOME

European badgers live together in groups of four to eight. Their burrows are much larger and have many entrances, tunnels, and chambers.

Chapter Three

LIFE INSIDE THE DEN

Badgers are mostly **nocturnal** and spend the day asleep in their dens. In summer, badgers don't always stay in the same burrow. Sometimes they dig a new one every day.

HOME SWEET HOME

Badgers back up into their dens if they feel threatened. They may also block the entrance with soil so nothing can get in.

Badgers sleep more in cold weather, so their winter dens tend to be larger. They usually choose one for the winter instead of changing every day. They may plug up part of the entrance with soil so the burrow stays warm inside.

The den where a female gives birth is also larger. It may have more than one chamber. The mother badger lines the **nursery** chamber with grass to keep the babies warm.

HOME SWEET HOME

Females give birth in March and have one to five babies. The young leave their mother for good when they're five to six months old.

Badgers often hunt by digging burrows. They're **carnivores** that eat **rodents** such as ground squirrels and mice. Badgers sniff out rodents' underground homes and tunnel in after them. They also eat rabbits, insects, and snakes.

Badgers also dig burrows to store food. These **caches** keep badgers' food hidden from other animals. The cooler underground temperatures also keep the food fresher.

HOME SWEET HOME

Badgers and coyotes sometimes hunt together. The coyote waits where a badger is burrowing to catch any rodents that run out.

Badgers live in dens all year, but some are always empty because badgers don't use the same one every day. That lets other animals like snakes, rabbits, and burrowing owls move in. Badger dens are homes for lots of creatures!

A LOOK INSIDE

GLOSSARY

burrows (bur-ohz) tunnels or holes in the ground used by an animal

caches (ka-shuz) hidden storage spaces

carnivores (kahr-nuh-vorz) animals that eat meat

chamber (chaym-bur) a room

nocturnal (nahk-tur-nuhl) active at night

nursery (nur-sur-ee) a place to raise babies

rodents (roh-duhnts) mammals with large front teeth that are constantly growing and used for gnawing things

solitary (sah-li-ter-ee) living or being on one's own

FURTHER READING

Koster, Gloria. *Coyotes and Badgers Team Up!* Capstone Press, 2023.

Ruby, Rex. *Inside a Badger's Burrow.* Bearport Publishing Company, 2023.

ON THE INTERNET

American Badger

www.nationalgeographic.com/animals/mammals/facts/american-badger

National Geographic tells you what American badgers look like, what they eat, and more.

Badger

https://kids.britannica.com/kids/article/badger/352815

Learn about different kinds of badgers and where they live with Britannica Kids.

INDEX